Original title:
Fronds of Fancy

Copyright © 2025 Creative Arts Management OÜ
All rights reserved.

Author: Eleanor Prescott
ISBN HARDBACK: 978-1-80567-329-3
ISBN PAPERBACK: 978-1-80567-628-7

Palms of Possibility

Beneath the shade of silly trees,
Laughter dances on the breeze.
A squirrel juggles nuts with glee,
While birds wear hats, just wait and see.

The sun is tickling my toes,
A lizard's wearing fancy clothes.
With every rustle, joy is found,
In this quirky world, I'm spellbound.

Tides of Emerald Dreams

Rolling waves of laughter swell,
A crab insists on showing its shell.
Seagulls gossip, what a sight,
As fish dive deep from morning light.

A jellyfish floats, quite a tease,
While seaweed sways like it's at ease.
In this ocean where humor flows,
Life's a splash, and laughter grows.

The Garden of Whimsy

Petunias dance in polka dots,
And daisies tell the silliest plots.
Veggies wearing sunglasses cool,
In this garden, humor's the rule.

Bumblebees hum a merry song,
While worms wiggle all day long.
Every bloom has a tale to weave,
In this patch where giggles never leave.

Lattice of Lushness

Vines entwine with a playful cheer,
A raccoon is having a cold beer.
Overhead, a parrot tells a joke,
As the flowers giggle and smoke.

The garden's a stage for ridiculous sights,
With ladybugs hosting kite-flying nights.
Each leaf bursts forth with a chuckle and grin,
In this vibrant space, let the fun begin!

Recollected Dreams of the Forest

In the woods where the squirrels prance,
Mushrooms dance with a silly stance.
Flowers giggle in bright attire,
As trees gossip by the green choir.

A raccoon makes a toast to the moon,
While owls hoot a quirky tune.
Bunnies bounce with a playful cheer,
Whispering secrets to the deer.

Sunbeams tickle the leaves on high,
While a turtle sings a lullaby.
The brook chuckles as it flows,
With fish that boast of their new clothes.

In this realm of whimsy and jest,
Every creature knows how to fest.
A parade of shadows in the night,
With laughter echoing in pure delight.

Leafy Lullabies of the Forest

In the grove where giggles sway,
Trees tell tales in a leafy play.
Squirrels dance on branches high,
As sunlight winks and the shadows sigh.

Mice wear hats made of acorn caps,
Holding tea parties on mossy laps.
Frogs croak tunes, a croaky choir,
While the wind strums leaves like a lyre.

Dreams Woven in Green Shadows

In green dreams where the daisies scheme,
Butterflies flutter with a silly beam.
Toadstools nod with a hefty grin,
As fireflies waltz, let the fun begin!

Bumblebees buzz in a zany flight,
Juggling pollen till the sun's goodnight.
The willow whispers funny jokes,
Whilst rabbits chuckle amid the oaks.

Cascades of Nature's Grace

Waterfalls flow with a playful splash,
As fish make faces in a wild dash.
Rocks giggle when fairies stomp,
And tree trunks sway with a happy romp.

Crickets chirp in a rhythm so bright,
Chatting secrets till the night.
The clouds make shapes of silly delight,
Tickling leaves in soft twilight.

Soft Echoes from Canopy Heights

High above in the leafy maze,
Birds share puns as they crisscross ways.
A squirrel slicks back its fuzzy hair,
While tree tops giggle without a care.

With acorn hats and twiggy shoes,
The forest sings of its goofy muse.
In this realm where smiles take flight,
Laughter lurks in the fading light.

Nature's Silken Embrace

In the garden where giggles grow,
Wiggly worms dance, putting on a show.
Butterflies waltz, a riot of hues,
While daisies gossip in colorful shoes.

Raindrops chuckle on cuddly grass,
Mice don tiny hats for all that sass.
Trees wear their grandeur, all puffy and proud,
As squirrels tell stories to the laughing crowd.

Echoing Laughter of the Leaves

Leaves swirl and twirl, a merry sight,
They whisper secrets in the warm sunlight.
Chirping birds fail in their choir,
As bees buzz by, chock-full of desire.

A leaf did a jig, while another just spun,
With every breeze, they're having such fun.
Nature's jesters play in splendid loops,
While rabbits grin in their leafy troops.

Impressions in Mossy Hues

Moss carpets the ground, soft and serene,
Making all footprints a bouncy routine.
Toadstools join in with their own little jig,
Crickets chime in with a raucous gig.

Squirrels wear glasses, pretending to read,
As mushrooms gather for a storytelling breed.
Each little creature, a humorous mate,
Life in the forest, a joyous fate.

Enchantment in Every Leaf

Each leaf waves hello with a shimmy and shake,
While spiders make jokes with their silken break.
A tree trunk grins with its gnarled old face,
Inviting all critters to join in the race.

With every rustle, a tickle in the air,
Nature's a comedian, with humor to spare.
In the heart of the woods, laughter takes flight,
As day turns to dusk, oh what a delight!

The Forest's Lyrical Embrace

In leafy hats, the squirrels play,
They dance around, no care, hooray!
With acorns flying through the air,
The forest chuckles, full of flair.

The trees wear coats of vibrant green,
Beneath the sun, they shine, a scene.
A rabbit hops, a wiggle here,
The birds all chirp, it's quite the cheer.

A deer does twirl, a marvelous sight,
While turtles turtle-walk with might.
With every step, the forest gleams,
It's all a part of nature's dreams.

In laughter loud, the winds comply,
As leafy giggles fill the sky.
With crazy spins, the branches bend,
This woodland joy has no clear end.

Green Symphony of the Soul

Notes of green, with a twist or two,
On branches high, the vines all coo.
The fox joins in with a woof so bold,
While mushrooms chuckle, secrets told.

A band of bugs in hats so wide,
Play lively songs, they do not hide.
The sapling sways to a beat so grand,
While dancing flowers lend a hand.

Old owls wink with a knowing grin,
As raccoons sport a silver tin.
The melody drifts through the air,
In harmony, they jump and stare.

Each leaf flutters like a soft cheer,
In this wild orchestra, all things dear.
A hilarious tune where all reside,
Nature's party, come join the ride!

Scattered Dreams Among the Branches

Up high, a dream is hung with care,
A cat on a cloud, she's lost in air.
With flying fish now tagging along,
A whimsical tale, forever strong.

The winds whisper jokes, a playful tease,
While ants in line march with great ease.
A grasshopper hops, wearing a hat,
He brews up laughter, imagine that!

Clouds morph forms, a dog, or perhaps,
A whole parade of colorful caps.
The branches sway with mischief's call,
In this playful realm, humor's the thrall.

Kid quirks in trees, all giggles and glee,
With dreams all scattered, wild and free.
They swing from hopes like swings in flight,
This laughter drift, a pure delight!

Murmurs in the Thicket

A gnome sings softly, lost in thought,
Creating smiles, which can't be bought.
The bushes chuckle, a rustling tune,
While insects dance beneath the moon.

A fox tells tales of past night's feast,
While frogs in tuxes croak like a beast.
With whispers low, the flowers blush,
Nature's gossip in a gentle hush.

Each twig a secret, each leaf a laugh,
In this tale-telling, there's no staff.
The thicket thrives with banter true,
As green companions create the brew.

When sun dips low, the laughter flows,
With silly quips, the night bestows.
In murmurs soft, the stories cling,
A vibrant jest to all they bring.

Beneath the Lush Embrace

In the shade of the leafy crown,
A squirrel tried on a paper gown.
He twirled and danced with such delight,
Mistaking a branch for a spotlight.

The daisies whispered tales of cheer,
As butterflies giggled, drawing near.
With buzzing bees adding their own tune,
A waltz in the garden, beneath the moon.

Fragments of Flora's Charm

A cactus wore a festive hat,
While tulips smiled and fed a cat.
The roses laughed, oh what a sight,
As petals plotted a bouncy flight.

A daffodil juggled drops of rain,
While violets sang of love and pain.
With each little bud, a chuckle grew,
Nature's gags, oh so true.

Weaving Nature's Wonders

A fern and a tree held hands in jest,
While a crow declared, 'I am the best!'
The vines creaked with laughter so bold,
　Telling stories that never grow old.

Grasshoppers joined in a song so sweet,
　With crickets tapping their tiny feet.
　They danced on leaves, all a-quiver,
Chasing the clouds that flowed down the river.

Breezes that Carry Secrets

The wind whispered jokes to the dandelions,
As they chuckled and tossed tiny ions.
A pine tree sighed, 'Would you rather be,
A bird that sings or a bee that's free?'

Nearby, an acorn rolled with glee,
Declaring, 'I dream of a big oak tree!'
With laughter swirling through the air,
Nature's humor found everywhere.

A Path Through Leafy Thoughts

In the woods where giggles grow,
Trees wear hats made of rainbow glow.
Squirrels dance in tiny shoes,
While singing songs of silly blues.

A raccoon juggles acorns bright,
Underneath a starry night.
With critters all in fun parade,
Their laughter weaves a leafy braid.

Chirping birds in silly bands,
Play the tunes of merry lands.
Every leaf a playful muse,
In nature's plot, no chance to snooze.

As the sun begins to fade,
Laughter spills in leafy shade.
On this path of whimsy's grace,
Joyful hearts find their place.

Fabric of Nature's Dreams

Seams of grass and thread of breeze,
Stitching stories with such ease.
A hedgehog dons a patchwork hat,
As dancing fireflies say 'cheers' to that!

The clouds wear cloaks of cotton fluff,
While mushrooms giggle, oh so tough.
Butterflies, they pirouette,
In a waltz, no regrets!

A tapestry of moments bright,
Sewn with laughter, pure delight.
Nature spins a silly yarn,
In every twist, a playful charm.

At dusk, the moon joins in the fun,
Winking down at everyone.
In this fabric, joy's the theme,
We weave together, dream by dream.

Sprouts of Creative Lullabies

Little sprouts with dreams to sing,
Humming tunes of everything.
Bunnies tapping tiny feet,
Dancing circles, oh so sweet!

Each petal tells a tale untold,
Whispers of joy, pure as gold.
With starlit eyes and cheeky grins,
The nighttime fun is where it begins.

Mice in pajamas take the stage,
As crickets chirp, their songs engage.
A world alive with giggles bright,
In cozy corners of the night.

These lullabies, they softly weave,
Dreams near trees, where we believe.
And when the day returns with light,
Joy still sprout, taking flight.

Whirlwinds of Leafy Joy

A gust comes rumbling through the trees,
Twirling leaves like giggling bees.
A jolly jog of grasses green,
Spins around in joyous sheen.

Chipmunks wear a joyful grin,
As breezes dance, they join in.
Nature's laughter fills the air,
What a view beyond compare!

With every whirl, a chuckle grows,
As blossoms giggle in rows.
Dandelions take a chance,
A wild and wiggly, windy dance!

As the sky begins to twirl,
Nature spins a joyful swirl.
In this whirlwind, fun's the guide,
Where laughter flows and dreams abide.

Spirals of Hope in the Breeze

In the garden, twirls and spins,
Silly blossoms tease and grin.
A tumbleweed in jest takes flight,
Chasing shadows, oh what a sight!

Bouncy birds hop on the line,
Squawking songs, a party divine.
The daisies dance with great delight,
As butterflies join in the light.

Enchanted by the Whispering Boughs

The trees gossip, what a thrill,
With giggles, they fulfill the will.
A squirrel winks, it's quite absurd,
As branches sway without a word.

Leaves rustle like a cheeky chat,
Telling tales of where it's at.
The breeze carries their whims so clear,
And tickles noses, brings good cheer!

Petals of Daydreams

In a land where wishes bloom,
A daffodil dances in a room.
A lily leaps with glee and grace,
While dandelions paint the space.

Swaying with laughter, petals fly,
Sprinkling joy in the big, blue sky.
A tulip trips and starts to roll,
Spreading mirth with playful soul.

Sylvan Secrets

Amid the woods, where laughter's shy,
The rabbits wear a comical tie.
They dance with joy, so wild and free,
Whispers rustle through each tree.

A hedgehog juggles acorns with flair,
While foxes giggle without a care.
In this realm, mischief is the game,
With every step, a new claim to fame!

Tangle of Life's Whims on Green

In a garden so wild and free,
The daisies danced with glee.
A squirrel wore a tiny hat,
And stole the pie from a sleeping cat.

The broccoli broke into a jig,
While carrots twirled, feeling big.
A cabbage rolled down the hill,
Shouting, 'Life's a thrill, what a thrill!'

Underneath a sunbeam's glance,
The peas began to prance.
With every leaf, a laugh to share,
In this patch, there's joy everywhere!

So here's to gardens, strange and bright,
Where whims take flight in sheer delight.
A tangle of joy, a sprinkle of cheer,
Nature's comedy unfolds right here.

Whirls of Flora and Fauna

In a grove where the blossoms play,
A gumdrop tree grew bright as day.
With tendrils twisting like a snake,
The flowers make silly shapes, oh what a break!

Bees wore shades, looking quite cool,
While butterflies danced around the pool.
A shy little fern tried to join in,
But tripped on a root—oh, what a win!

The tulips giggled, heads held high,
As a woodchuck claimed the sky.
With a quack and a wiggle, they trumped the rules,
In a world full of laughter, aren't plants the best fools?

Each petal spins a tale so bright,
In nature's ruckus, all feels right.
Whirls of flora in playful disguise,
They spread joy with each surprise.

The Artistry of Dappled Delight

Beneath a tree, I spy a sight,
A gopher painting day and night.
With berries squished, a palette true,
He makes the grass look fresh and new.

The sunbeams tickle leaves awake,
While bushy tails shake, oh what a break!
A hedgehog recites a lopsided rhyme,
As daisies sway in sync with time.

Each flower poses, a model grand,
In this whimsical, leafy band.
With laughter hidden in every bloom,
Nature's laughter fills the room.

Artistry in every shade and hue,
Where quirky creatures indulge anew.
Delightful antics dance in the light,
As nature stirs in pure delight.

Whispers of the Greenery

In whispers soft, the ivy speaks,
Of silly chats and playful peaks.
A cricket's laugh, a worm's ballet,
In this leafy theatre, they come out to play.

The mushrooms giggle, tops held high,
While spiders weave under the sky.
A dandelion starts a conga line,
As ants applaud, saying, 'That's just fine!'

The bamboo sways, a dancer bold,
Telling secrets that never grow old.
While lilacs blush, feeling quite coy,
Every petal hums, 'Oh what a joy!'

So listen close to the rustling leaves,
A symphony of nature that never deceives.
In whispers of greenery, laughter spreads,
Life's witty tales are what nature threads.

Between the Leaves of Creation

In the garden, jokes do bloom,
Laughter dances, chasing gloom.
Petals chuckle in the breeze,
Whispers tease the buzzing bees.

Trees wear hats of leafy green,
Squirrels share their circus scene.
Gnomes in corners laugh aloud,
Napping 'neath a joyful cloud.

Roots are tangled in a twist,
Worms tell tales that can't be missed.
Sunbeams giggle down the lane,
Dancing lightly, full of plain.

In this plush, comedic land,
Nature's humor, close at hand.
Each laugh shared, a leaf unfurled,
Moment's joy, a happy world.

Chants of the Overhead Sky

Clouds wear costumes, fluffy and bright,
They bounce and play, quite a sight.
Raindrops drum like silly tunes,
Making merry with the moons.

Birds in chorus chirp their song,
Flapping wings, they play along.
Witty winds weave through the trees,
Carrying giggles on the breeze.

Sunshine pokes its cheerful face,
Tickling shadows in this space.
Stars at night, in winks and blinks,
Share their cosmic, silly kinks.

Nightlights twinkle in delight,
The sky giggles, pure starlight.
Nature's humor, bold and free,
Chants of joy, eternally.

The Verdant Tapestry

Leaves are ribbons, green and bright,
Swaying gently, full of light.
Stitches made of sun and shade,
In this quilt, fun is laid.

Flowers jump in colors rare,
Winking at the passer's stare.
Buzzing bees bring punchlines sweet,
Tickling pollen, think on feet.

Grass blades tickle toes that roam,
Each step feels like being home.
A crooked path of giggles plays,
Laughter lingers through the days.

This tapestry, rich and bold,
Hides its humor, bright and gold.
Nature's whimsy all around,
In every leaf, a laugh is found.

Flora's Hidden Poetry

In every petal, words take flight,
Whispers spun in morning light.
Daisies giggle, tulips dance,
Nature writes with sweet romance.

Vines entwine in playful fun,
Tickling branches till they run.
A garden full of silly prose,
In every tree and blooming rose.

Mushrooms caper, small and round,
Hosting parties underground.
Earthworms tell their tales of yore,
While critters bicker, wanting more.

Poetry blooms in every scene,
Insects join the book routine.
Nature's laugh, a secret found,
In leafy verses, joy is crowned.

Whispers of Verdant Dreams

In a garden where giggles play,
The flowers wear hats all day.
Tulips gossip, daisies tease,
While squirrels juggle with such ease.

Bees in tuxedos buzz with flair,
Pollen parties fill the air.
With petals dancing, oh so bright,
They twirl and swirl in pure delight.

Lush Secrets in the Breeze

The ivy whispers silly tales,
As lizards sport their tiny sails.
Butterflies with polka dots
Make friends with frogs in funny spots.

Grasshoppers strum a tune or two,
While worms do the cha-cha, oh so true.
Each leaf a dancer, quick and spry,
In this lush realm, they leap and fly.

Dance of the Emerald Veils

Underneath the leafy hue,
Caterpillars play peek-a-boo.
With twirls and spins, they sway and glide,
Emerald veils in a laughter ride.

A snail wearing glasses takes the lead,
While ants march like a parade indeed.
Sunlight twinkles, a playful tease,
As the garden giggles with sweet ease.

Petals and Feathers entwined

Petals laugh when feathers fall,
A tickle fight, a gentle brawl.
Parrots joke with blooms nearby,
In a colorful spectacle, oh my!

A daisy's crown with a quirk or two,
As cockatoos dance, how they flew.
With a chirp, a swoosh, and a flutter,
Nature's comedy, a joyful clutter.

Shadows of the Canopy's Heart

In a tree, a squirrel took a nap,
Woke up to find his acorn cap.
He scratched his head and looked around,
For nuts were nowhere to be found.

An owl flew in, gave a hoot,
Said, "Try the vines, they might bear fruit!"
The squirrel grinned, with a little hop,
To dine on greens, he'd never stop.

As sunlight danced, a playful breeze,
Unraveled secrets from the leaves.
The squirrel laughed, in shades of green,
Who knew his home could feel so keen?

Now shadows twirl with silly tricks,
The critters laugh, what a funny mix!
In the canopy, joy takes flight,
A silly dance ever so bright.

Tales Beneath the Lush Arches

Beneath the leaves, a rabbit pranced,
With hops so bold, he looked entranced.
He thought he heard a tale unfold,
From twinkle toes, to tails of gold.

A fox nearby began to cheer,
"Do tuck and roll, my friend, come here!"
They spun and leapt, in soft delight,
While sunshine sparkled, oh what a sight!

With every dance, a giggle grew,
The trees leaned in, oh yes, it's true!
They whispered tales of days gone past,
Where laughter echoed, wild and fast.

So here they play, in charming show,
Twisting tales, just feel that flow!
Beneath the arches, joy takes wing,
A merry heart makes shadows sing.

The Choreography of Ferns in the Wind

Wiggly ferns in frenzied twirl,
Dance with leaves, and flags unfurl.
A breeze blew in, a sudden push,
And grasshoppers joined, with a big whoosh!

The ladybugs in polka dots,
Joined the fun, or maybe not.
They twirled around, and spun in place,
With flutters and giggles, what a race!

The ferns said, "Hey, come join our spree!"
While butterflies danced, so wild and free.
In the rhythm of nature's glee,
There's hope and laughter as friends decree.

Together they sway, in a leafy groove,
Each silly jig, a playful move.
In the wind, they find their zest,
Nature's festival, it's for the best!

Secrets Splayed in Sun-dappled Light

In sunbeams bright, the brightness spills,
A turtle winks, a squirrel thrills.
They set to ponder secrets bright,
In dappled realms, such pure delight.

"I lost my hat!" the turtle sighed,
"In the pond, I took a ride!"
The squirrel chuckled, "What a sight!
I'll fetch it, don't you worry, right?"

Underneath the green-laced sky,
Mischief happens, oh my, oh my!
They scrabble, tumble, trip and glide,
In beams of laughter, none can hide.

With each riddle tucked away,
Nature whispers, "Come and play!"
In the secrets warmed by day's embrace,
A funny twist in this leafy space.

Canopied Journeys

Under the green, where critters play,
Squirrels converse in a comical way.
Leaves whisper secrets, oh what a tease,
Gardens giggle beneath the tall trees.

Toads wear crowns made of flower pot tops,
Wobbling dance steps and laugh till it stops.
Butterflies chuckle as they flit about,
Join in the riddle, come see what it's about.

In this world where the sunlight beams,
Tangles of laughter blend with our dreams.
Chasing the shadows, a playful parade,
Every wild turn is a joyous escapade.

Botanical Fantasia

Petals in pajama, oh what a sight,
Roses are rolling, such jolly delight!
Daisies do cartwheels, tulips in line,
Gardening gnomes sip tea, oh how divine!

Vines intertwine in a ticklish way,
Bouncing along like they're here to play.
Bees in tuxedos, buzzing a tune,
Dancing, they'll party 'neath the full moon.

Whimsical leaves in a merry parade,
Tickled by breezes that never do fade.
Nature's a jester, delightfully bright,
Laughter and colors, a whimsical sight!

Silhouettes of Serenity

Shadows are chuckling as dusk starts to fall,
Mice in top hats start their own ball.
Owls hoot in rhythm, a wise guy's grin,
Stars blink in jest, let the fun begin!

Bats in the background, doing the twist,
Who knew nighttime could be so blissed?
Pillows of clouds, fluffy as dreams,
Floating on laughter, nothing is as it seems.

Calmness and chaos in perfect embrace,
The moon shares a joke, lighting up space.
Dance with the night, and sing with the day,
In the funny shadows where we love to play.

Leafy Lullabies

Crickets compose tunes that whisk us away,
In cozy leaf beds, we're ready to sway.
Singing to stars in the gentle night air,
Whispers of leaves with a tickle to share.

Laughter trickles down like a soft rain,
As fireflies twinkle, it's never mundane.
Frogs put on plays with a jump and a croak,
Nature's our theater, come see the stroke!

Under the moon, the giggles resound,
In sleepy groves where the funny is found.
So drift into dreams where the wild things lay,
In leafy lullabies, we play and we play.

Dances in the Foliage

In the woods, the leaves all prance,
Swaying gently, they join the dance.
A cabbage whisper, a playful sneeze,
Laughter rustles through the trees.

A squirrel twirls in his tiny coat,
While lizards leap and goats emote.
A rabbit hops on a ladybug's back,
Together they form a travel pack.

The breeze giggles, the sun throws a wink,
Magic happens at the edge of the brink.
With every sway, the world feels brighter,
As leafy limbs become the fighters.

A jaunty tune from a bug-filled choir,
Competes with the crackles of a frisky fire.
In the foliage, no rule is laid,
Where silly shadows become unafraid.

A Tangle of Imagination

Twisted vines with stories to tell,
Spin tales of where the pixies dwell.
The flowers giggle, the mushrooms tease,
It's a merry mess among the trees.

A butterfly slips on a fancy shoe,
While ants parade in a grand review.
The snails all blurt what they overheard,
In a language that pokes and prods absurd.

Mice discuss the latest fashion trend,
Appearing chic as they twirl and bend.
Nature's whispers buzz like spun gold thread,
As ideas bloom where few would tread.

In this wild maze of leafy delight,
Imagination dances like stars at night.
Each twist and turn is a giggly surprise,
Beneath the canopy sprawling skies.

Hidden Under Leafy Veils

Underneath the emerald shroud,
Giggles echo, bright and loud.
A frog leaps in a shimmering suit,
Hosting a ball, who would dispute?

Caterpillars boast of dreams ahead,
In cozy nooks where the berries spread.
A snail on a quest, slow but spry,
Searching for treasure where daydreams lie.

The sunbeams tickle, the shadows play,
Behind the leaves, the magic's at bay.
In the nooks of nature, silliness brews,
As characters frolic, singing the blues.

Mushrooms pop in their polka-dot suits,
While bees buzz in their tiny hoots.
Underneath the veil, mystery thrives,
Where laughter echoes and joy derives.

Nature's Tender Caress

In the garden, the giggles bloom,
With petals soft like a cozy room.
Buttercups whisper in sunny tones,
While sunflowers dance in silly zones.

A breeze tells stories of wild delight,
While ladybugs gather for a night flight.
The garden gnomes share their secret jokes,
With chuckles hidden amidst the oaks.

Frolicking ferns in colors bright,
Sprout laughter beneath the moonlight.
While crickets play their tiny tunes,
The night air shimmers like cartoon grooms.

Amidst cuddly weeds, life's fun unspools,
As critters gather in playful schools.
In this garden where silliness sways,
Nature's tender touch forever stays.

Lush Vistas Unveiled

In the garden of giggles, a tall plant swayed,
Pants made of lettuce made the squirrels afraid.
Birds wore bowties, so slick and so neat,
Each crumb they dropped, was their salad treat.

Laughter burst forth from the daisies' bloom,
As gnomes in the corner began to assume.
They danced on the lawn, in tap shoes of clay,
While the sun grinned wide, brightening the day.

Turtles in top hats, so dapper and proud,
Held a tea party, inviting the crowd.
With donuts and juice from the flowered vase,
They sipped with a spout while wearing a face.

Oh, what a sight, the odd jokes they wove,
Nature's own circus, no bounds, all in trove.
A tapestry woven with chuckles and cheer,
In this world of whimsy, it's perfectly clear.

Echoes Among the Leaves

Whispers of jokes from the shivering leaves,
As critters exchanged puns, the laughter achieves.
The cabbage took flight, with a cape made of green,
While the beets played the drums, like a vegetable scene.

A raccoon with spectacles read from a book,
Speaking of mysteries, come take a look!
The stones rolled their eyes, while the worms made a fuss,
Saying, "Your plot twists are making us blush!"

In the hush of the night, the crickets convened,\nTo plan a surprise: a dance so esteemed.
While shadows were slinking, the moon took a bow,
And all of the creatures joined in, somehow.

So here in the grove, with each rustle and sway,
Laughter and joy come to enhance the play.
As echoes of humor bounce off every trunk,
In the heart of the leaves, humor's never shrunk.

Dreaming in Canopy Shadows

Beneath tangled branches, a dream takes its flight,
With shadows that giggle, and stars shining bright.
A shadowy cat in a polka-dot hat,
Whispered secrets of gardens, where all the fun sat.

With a moonbeam's twirl, the owls would conspire,
To host a grand banquet, oh, how they'd aspire!
The guests were all fungi, in suits oh-so-merry,
As they danced to the tunes from a wise old berry.

In this land of delight, where the laughter won't stop,
The flowers played tag in a whimsical hop.
A puppet of vine told a joke with a snap,
And the frogs in the pond laughed in their nap.

With each fleeting dusk, when the sun kissed the leaves,
The fabric of night wraps all mischief it weaves.
For here in the hush, where the shadows do sway,
Life's playful wonders brightly hold sway.

Verdant Reveries

In the vale where the sillies and giggles unite,
A worm put on spectacles, claimed he could write.
With advice from a thistle on how to compose,
They penned a great book about garden woes.

The daisies wore crowns; the bees played the lute,
While the lilies cooked dinner, a marvelous fruit.
Each berry had secrets, they whispered and sighed,
While the grass tickled toes, converting the tide.

Oh, laughter cascaded like rain on the ferns,
As the beetles played chess and debated their turns.
With smiles made of sunshine and giggles on high,
In this vibrant fiesta, we could surely fly.

For nature's a theater, and we're here to play,
Where whimsy is woven, with joy on display.
Each critter a star in this fanciful scene,
In verdant reveries, nothing's ever routine.

Elysian Gardens Await

In gardens where the daisies dance,
A gnome attempts a clumsy prance.
He trips on weeds, oh what a sight,
While butterflies take off in flight.

The carrots wear their leafy hats,
As squirrels debate with chubby rats.
The sunflowers giggle, quite afar,
While chatting 'bout the latest star.

A turtle plays the ukulele tune,
While bumblebees buzz afternoon.
With laughter in this sunny glade,
No trouble here, just joy displayed.

So come and join this merry crew,
Where all things nutty blossom too.
In gardens filled with jokes and cheer,
With silly antics all the year.

Beneath the Boughs of Delight

Beneath the trees, the shadows play,
Where chipmunks toss their acorns stray.
A parrot squawks, so loud and clear,
Declaring all its jokes, oh dear!

The mushrooms wear their polka dots,
And tease the frogs who tie their knots.
While owls make faces, wise and round,
In this odd circus so profound.

A rabbit juggles carrots wide,
As hedgehogs cheer from side to side.
They laugh so hard, they start to roll,
As nature swirls, it steals the show.

So take a seat on grass so green,
Join in the fun, it's quite the scene.
With each silly giggle intertwined,
We'll leave our cares and woes behind.

Mysteries of the Canopy

In leafy heights, the secrets peek,
As monkeys dance and squirrels sneak.
With laughter echoing from above,
While birds exchange their tales of love.

The branches sway, they tip and twirl,
As butterflies make quite a whirl.
A beetle dons a shiny tie,
While thinking how to touch the sky.

Such mysteries under blooms so bright,
Where every turn brings pure delight.
In this grand show, we all partake,
With nature's quirks, make no mistake!

Come share the giggles, join the spree,
As flowers bloom with wild glee.
Beneath the branches, let's explore,
The funny side of nature's lore.

Nature's Embrace Engraved

In nature's grip, the laughter soars,
As frogs perform on lily floors.
A hedgehog's flip, oh what a sight,
With every burp, it takes the flight!

Around the pond, the ducks parade,
In wacky hats, they join the trade.
With silly quacks and wristwatches askew,
They set the stage for laugh anew.

The trees will chuckle, their leaves all shake,
As fireflies play hide and seek, awake.
With nature's script, the scenes unfold,
In witty tales that never grow old.

So gather 'round, my friends, my pals,
Where whimsy lives and laughter prowls.
In nature's arms, let humor thrive,
As we embrace the joy, alive!

Verdant Reveries of the Wild

In a jungle where the geese wear shoes,
The squirrels gossip, sharing wild news.
Llamas dance, with hats on their heads,
While grasshoppers dream in their leafy beds.

The trees do twist in a waltzing spree,
As mushrooms play cards with a bumblebee.
Frogs wear ties and start a debate,
Who sings better, the owl or the crate?

A deer in a scarf takes a stroll by the brook,
While fish read novels in a well-worn nook.
The flowers giggle and sway in the breeze,
As playful ants throw a party with cheese.

Laughter rings out from the thicket so dense,
A fox tells tales that don't make much sense.
With whimsy and wit, nature's light heart,
In this wild, funny world, all play their part.

The Symphony of Leafy Dreams

In a choir of leaves, the trees all sing,
About rocky romances and pollen bling.
A raccoon in tights performs a grand show,
While butterflies flutter through gardens aglow.

The breeze plays the flute, so tender and sweet,
As daisies tap dance with whimsical feet.
A ladybug conducts with a glittery wand,
As crazy crickets play on and respond.

An owl in glasses reads poetry aloud,
Keeping the crowd of critters quite proud.
The sunbeams chuckle, tickling the sky,
As laughter echoes, and time flies by.

In this leafy symphony of giggles and joy,
Where every critter's a playful decoy.
Nature's own orchestra, light-hearted tunes,
Setting the stage for vibrant afternoons.

Unfurling Stories in Sunlit Spaces

In sunlit corners where shadows play peek,
The toadstools whisper what the daisies speak.
Bumblebees wear coats and tip their hats,
While jumpy frogs recite jokes to the cats.

A sunflower winks with a radiant grin,
While ants throw confetti for the ants' kin.
A breeze carries laughter under the trees,
Where nature's mischief puts minds at ease.

The sky's a blue canvas where clouds make art,
With strokes of humor they don't take to heart.
A picnic with giggles, the critters all feast,\nAs cabbage rolls out the leafy-based beast.

In these sunlit spaces, enchantments flow,
Stories unfold in a comical show.
With every petal and flurry of flight,
Nature's tales burst into joyous delight.

Nature's Brush Against Time

With strokes of green that dance and delight,
Nature takes canvas, vibrant and bright.
A playful pelican twirls by the shore,
While seagulls tell secrets, wanting to soar.

The sun casts shadows that twist and tease,
As crickets recite their nightly decrees.
Trees paint whispers of laughter and cheer,
While squirrels debate whose nap time is near.

In circular patterns, grass blades engage,
Witty remarks from the pond's little sage.
The moon smiles wide as the stars throw a ball,
In nature's art gallery, we all hear the call.

With a swish of her brush, time bows low,
To the quirky creations that ebb and flow.
In hilarious hues, life's canvas is spun,
Painting our laughter 'til the day's done.

The Alchemy of Leaves

In a whirl of color, the leaves conspire,
Crafting potions of laughter, never to tire.
They dance on the breeze, oh what a sight,
Turning dull afternoons into pure delight.

With whispers of mischief across sunny glades,
They tickle the branches with cheeky charades.
The squirrels take notes, with bushes as desks,
While the flowers giggle, avoiding the texts.

A leaf once declared, with a twinkle and tease,
"I'm not just a plant—they've made me a breeze!"
Nature's grand jest when the sun starts to fade,
Leaves chuckle together, too funny to trade.

As night falls gently, the shadows begin,
The laughter of foliage is never quite thin.
They plan mischief anew when dawn's light arrives,
For amongst the green, the joy truly thrives.

Enigma in the Garden

In a patch of green where the cacti wear hats,
Mysterious whispers from the chattering gats.
Flowers exchange secrets in colorful tones,
And the earthworms gossip of their delightful zones.

Bees don little jackets, buzz cluelessly bold,
While daisies unveil tales that were never told.
The sun chuckles brightly, casting shadows of fun,
As laughter erupts in the land of the sun.

The carrots are gossiping over a drink,
The radishes giggle, unable to think.
Amid summer's delight, there's a raucous parade,
Each bloom a comedian, no act ever strayed.

The garden's a stage, with applause from the breeze,
A riddle of joyful foliage dancing with ease.
In this mirthful enclave, where humor is found,
The punchlines grow wild, with laughter unbound.

Fillings of the Elysium Grove

In the grove where the yolks of the sun come to play,
Each nut and each berry has something to say.
Cherries wear giggles, prancing with zest,
While mushrooms concoct a whimsical fest.

Pine cones gossip about fall's upcoming show,
With rumors of squirrels who put on a glow.
The elderflowers plot from their thicket so snug,
While bees replicate moves in a well-aimed mug.

Overhead, the branches of oak and of pine,
They forge silly stories, divine and benign.
With saplings intertwining in hapless romance,
Each dandelion teases to leap and to dance.

As dusk brings a hush to the leafy delight,
The stars wink knowingly, turning day into night.
Inside this grand grove where the fun never sways,
They host wild banquets of laughter-filled days.

Explorations in the Green Realm

In a kingdom of foliage, a quest has begun,
With thickets and mazes, oh what fun!
The flowers hold maps with color so bold,
Each petal a clue to the stories retold.

With a giggly wind leading paths of surprise,
The bushes are plotting, with mischievous eyes.
The daisies, they wager on who finds the prize,
While dragons made of ivy begin to arise.

Each leaf is a jester, each twig a wise sage,
In this tapestry green, the laughter's the wage.
The ferns whisper secrets that tickle your ear,
As the sweet scent of dewdrops renders you cheer.

In this realm of green wonders, adventure is key,
Where mischief and joy fill the air like a spree.
So come join the frolic, a fantastical dream,
For exploring this haven is all that it seems.

Shadows of Sunlit Dreams

In the garden where giggles bloom,
Laughter dances with the broom.
Flowers wear spectacles, quite absurd,
As bees recite the silliest word.

A snail in a hat, what a sight!
Hitching a ride on a bug's back flight.
The sun throws tantrums, hiding its rays,
While daisies tell jokes in sunlit displays.

Caresses of the Caressing Wind

The wind tickles trees, such a tease,
Whispers secrets to buzzing bees.
Leaves join in a cheeky ballet,
As squirrels giggle their worries away.

Clouds wear mustaches, all in good fun,
A playful race, the clouds always run.
They trip on laughter, bounce off of light,
As nature laughs at the curious sight.

Palette of the Earthbound Muse

Colors splash across the ground,
The grass paints stories, to be found.
Roses blush, wearing silly grins,
While daisies poke fun at their spins.

A painter of mischief, the sky holds the brush,
As puddles giggle in a cheerful hush.
Each hue a chuckle, each shade a jest,
Nature's canvas is humorously blessed.

Grove of Unspoken Fantasies

In a grove where whispers collide,
Trees chuckle at secrets they hide.
A rabbit with spectacles reads a book,
While owls swoop in, just to look.

Branches are tickled by unknown hands,
As shadows play in whimsical bands.
The air is thick with giggles and bliss,
Nature's comedy, none should miss.

Tender Twists of Greenery

In a garden bright, with colors so keen,
Plants tell secrets, they wander and preen.
A dandelion's giggle, a leaf's playful dance,
In nature's stage, everybody gets a chance.

Beneath the moonlight, shadows take flight,
A cactus in jest wears a hat just right.
Roses roll laughter, thorns chuckle with glee,
In this leafy kingdom, it's all fun, you see!

One fern is a joker, with tricks up its sleeve,
While daisies are gossiping, hard to believe.
Each flower a character, wild and absurd,
A comedy show where the petals are heard.

So come join the laughter, plant a smile wide,
In this green universe, let joy be our guide.
With vines that are silly and blooms that can sing,
Together we'll dance, as the foliage swings.

Flourishing Inspirations

Underneath the sun, where the whimsy agrees,
Petunias wear sunglasses, swaying with ease.
Rabbits recite poetry, squirrels tap dance,
In the garden of giggles, we all take a chance.

The lettuce is laughing, its jokes quite a thrill,
While herbs share their secrets, a gourmet's goodwill.
Carrots tell tales of the deep underground,
Where radishes rumble, and laughter abounds.

A sunflower winks, its face to the sky,
While whispers of flora float gently nearby.
It's a party of colors, a festival bright,
Where petals and leaves mix with pure delight.

So gather your joy, let your heart take a leap,
In this garden of fun, where laughter runs deep.
Nature's the canvas, and we are the brush,
Creating with smiles, in a whimsical hush.

Swaying with the Soft Wind

Swinging and swaying, where breezes collide,
A chorus of voices from each leafy side.
The willows are whispering, hints of a jest,
As daisies poke fun at the sun's silly quest.

Bamboo is gossiping, telling wild tales,
While ferns sway along, like they're on ocean gales.
Grasshoppers raving with hops full of glee,
Dance parties erupt in the shade of the tree.

A butterfly giggles, a caterpillar spins,
As pollen sings sweetly, where mischief begins.
The petals are chatting, the stems throwing shade,
In this humorous garden, no joy is delayed.

Join in the frolic, let laughter unwind,
With nature as our stage, and the breeze as our mind.
We'll sway with the soft wind, dance till the night,
In a whimsical world, everything feels right.

Layers of Dreamweaving

In layers of color, where laughter unfolds,
Each petal a story, each stem love that holds.
Grapevines converse, in whispers, they play,
While neighbors, the daisies, throw shade in their way.

The garden's alive with a comical twist,
As marigolds prance, in sunlight they twist.
Cabbages chuckle at the silly old squash,
And rhubarb with humor throws a bright quash.

Beneath playful clouds, where the sunshine does peek,
Tulips are teasing, in colors they speak.
Nature's a jester, with blooms that will sing,
Layered in laughter, it's a joyous swing.

So take off your shoes, and dance on the green,
In a patchwork of joy, where all can be seen.
We'll weave through the layers, let imagination soar,
In this playful garden, forever adored.

Rhythms of Rooted Whispers

In the garden, plants a-chatter,
Wiggly roots, what's the matter?
They gossip down in tangled lines,
Sharing secrets 'neath the pines.

Beneath the soil, they tap their toes,
To disco beats that no one knows.
With leafy hats and muddy shoes,
They dance away the morning blues.

While daisies giggle, and grasses sway,
The daisies promise to not betray.
But when a breeze starts tickling stems,
They burst out laughing like wild gems.

So let them whisper, let them sing,
The roots, they know the funniest thing.
In the soil where we can't peek,
They party on, and never speak!

Dance of the Waving Palms

Oh the palms, they sway so proud,
In the sun, they shout out loud.
With fronds that flop and greet the sky,
They wave to each passerby.

On tropical shores, they twist and turn,
With every gust, they laugh and yearn.
They spin around, a leafy whirl,
In their own palm tree ballet, they twirl.

Beneath the sun, they pull a prank,
A shadow play on the beachy bank.
With rustling leaves, they sing a tune,
As seagulls dance beneath the moon.

So here's to palms and their crazy fun,
Shaking their fronds under the sun.
Join their dance, you won't regret,
For in this grove, no one is fret!

Luminescence in Leaf Shadows

In patchy glades where sunlight beams,
The leaves are plotting in their dreams.
Chatting softly, tossing shade,
Playing games in the glen they made.

Beneath a tree, a shadow glides,
Whispers of mischief in leafy hides.
Chasing bugs with leafy flair,
Who knew plants could dance and dare?

The sunlight giggles, casts a glow,
As friendly leaves begin to flow.
They flick to right, then to the left,
Spreading joy, a leafy theft.

What antics bloom in leafy nooks,
A world of fun beyond the books.
So tiptoe softly, join the play,
With shadows bright that lead the way!

Gemstones of Greenery

In the meadow, shiny spots,
Gems of green in tangled knots.
With colors bright, they laugh and gleam,
Sprinkling joy like a child's dream.

Clover glitters with dew drops bright,
A diamond dance in morning light.
They tease the bees, they sing along,
Nature's chorus, fun and strong.

Wildflowers giggle, a colorful crew,
Dressed in hues of every hue.
They sway with grace, a vibrant crew,
Making humor bloom anew.

So here's a toast to nature's glee,
To gemstones bright, wild, and free.
In gardens lush, let laughter reign,
With greenery's joy, we'll lose the pain!

A Tale of Twining Vines

In a garden lush, plants dance with delight,
Twisting around, they giggle each night.
A pumpkin once tripped, with pride he did boast,
While cucumbers whispered, "What a silly host!"

A sunflower winked, with petals so wide,
As tomatoes played peek-a-boo, full of pride.
The carrots stood tall, with green hats on high,
Laughing at beans as they waved goodbye.

There's mischief afoot in this colorful spree,
Where seedlings recite both the funny and free.
With roots intertwined, and humor to grow,
A tale of twining vines, always in flow.

Serenity in Bloom

In a meadow of giggles, blooms chuckle away,
Petals that flutter like they've come to play.
The daisies all gossip, their faces so bright,
They tickle the wind, what a hilarious sight!

The tulips are wearing their fanciest hats,
While bees hum a tune, they dance like acrobats.
At night, fireflies twinkle, join in the cheer,
A festival of laughter brings sunshine near.

Jokes linger sweetly, they float in the air,
A symphony of color, a joy we all share.
In this garden of giggles, worries take flight,
Serenity blooms in the soft, warm night.

Nature's Echoes and Elixirs

The leaves whisper secrets in breezes that play,
With twigs on a mission, they sway and they sway.
The frogs in the pond sing their croaky delight,
While turtles argue who'll win in a fight.

A squirrel stole acorns, thinking it's grand,
While birds chirp and gossip about all that's planned.
The nectar's so sweet, it makes bees do a jig,
As butterflies feel like they're up for a gig.

The laughter of nature is found all around,
In echoes and elixirs, fun surely abounds.
With joy in their hearts, creatures dance and they sing,
In this wild, wondrous world, where humor takes wing.

Lace of Nature's Imagination

Spiders spin stories with delicate thread,
Creating fine patterns, not a word left unsaid.
As ladybugs giggle on a leaf with a sigh,
They plot their next venture, oh my, oh my!

The clouds drift by softly, wearing a grin,
While picking the stars is where fun shall begin.
The grass tickles toes in a playful ballet,
And mushrooms provide a hilarious array.

So gather your laughter, let it take flight,
In this tapestry woven, both silly and bright.
With nature's grand laughter, let's join in the play,
In a lace of creation, come smile the day away.

The Tapestry of Nature's Breath

In the garden where giggles grow,
Trees dance around, putting on a show.
Bugs in suits with bow ties so neat,
Chirping symphonies with tapping feet.

Sunlight winks, the breeze gets cheeky,
Leaves laugh together, they're quite sneaky.
Petals jive in a yellow parade,
While shadows join in, unafraid.

Caterpillars wear hats made of dew,
Sipping sweet tea, oh what a view!
Nature's jesters in a playful spree,
Chasing the clouds, wild and free.

The earth's a stage, come take a seat,
Where each plant prances to nature's beat.
With every whisper, a giggle bends,
In this tapestry where the laughter lends.

Delicate Vines and Sunlit Glades

In the glade where shadows twine,
Vines weave tales with a twisty line.
Daisies play peek-a-boo with the sun,
While squirrels giggle, oh what fun!

Under bright skies, a circus bloom,
With petals that dance, dispelling gloom.
Frogs on leaves in a jovial hop,
Singing loudly, they'll never stop.

Bumblebees buzz like flying jesters,
Painting the air with their sweet festers.
Caterpillars wearing clownish hats,
Strut their stuff, while a butterfly chats.

Every rustle, a punchline brewed,
In lush green realms, joy is renewed.
Nature's laughter, a playful serenade,
Amidst the vines, friendships are made.

Flourish Under the Emerald Sky

Beneath the boughs where fun takes flight,
Laughter echoes through day and night.
Flowers giggle, their colors bright,
As squirrels juggle, what a sight!

Sunbeams dance on the mossy floor,
Tickling toes, asking for more.
Hares in hats play hopscotch wide,
While ladybugs take silly slides.

The emerald sky holds secrets tight,
As wind knows jokes till they feel right.
Roots chuckle softly, they've seen it all,
From whispers of raindrops to seasons' call.

In nature's stage, every creature has fun,
Under the gaze of the glowing sun.
With every bloom, the joy does fry,
In this patch of bliss beneath the sky.

Melody of the Sylvan Whispers

In the woods where giggles flit,
Trees echo back with a playful wit.
Branches sway, a game of tease,
While sounds of laughter ride the breeze.

Singing stones and chuckling streams,
Our forest friends share fanciful dreams.
Toads in cloaks tell tales of old,
While mischievous winds let secrets unfold.

Mushrooms popping like popcorn hot,
In this enchanted, silly plot.
Crickets perch, choosing the tune,
As they strum their strings beneath the moon.

Every rustle plays a melody,
Nature's orchestra, wild and free.
With each whisper, a joy that lingers,
In these woods where laughter's fingers.

Aviation of the Heart

In the sky, my heart takes flight,
With a paper plane, though it's not quite.
Clouds giggle as my dreams go by,
Catching the breeze with a silly sigh.

I tried to steer but got lost instead,
Bouncing on clouds, I almost fled.
Stars wink down, full of cheeky glee,
'Flying's a joke, come laugh with me!'

From the cockpit of my cereal bowl,
I'm a pilot of dreams, that's my goal.
Turbulence comes from Grandma's stew,
Yet I soar through skies of bright blue.

So pack a laugh, let worries depart,
Join me in this aviation of the heart!
With giggles as our guiding thread,
Up to the clouds, we joyfully tread.

Melody of the Garden

In the garden, tunes are sprouting,
With flowers singing, no doubt about it.
Bees dance in rhythm, a buzzing choir,
While daisies sway to their heart's desire.

The carrots hum a cheerful tune,
As the radishes glide like a cartoon.
A cabbage wobbles, can't keep the beat,
While a turnip twirls on two little feet.

Sunshine tickles each leaf and petal,
Creating giggles, oh what a settle!
With rain as applause, it falls from the sky,
Every drop a note that makes us laugh high.

So come and join this leafy parade,
Where laughter and music will never fade!
In the melody of this vibrant patch,
Even snails groove—oh, a perfect match!

Vines of Enchantment

In the window, a vine begins to creep,
With dreams of reaching the moon, not cheap.
It trips over pots, causing a mess,
Is it magic or did it just guess?

It whispers secrets to the dusty air,
Befriends a spider with a silly stare.
Together they plot, oh what a sight,
To dance in the moonlight, through the night.

Caterpillars giggle, sharing their views,
While the ivy tells jokes, just to amuse.
A snail on a leaf hums a soft tune,
As the sun peeks out, bright as a balloon.

So let these vines tell tales quite absurd,
Where giggles and whimsy are always heard.
In this charming tangle, full of delight,
Life's little mess-ups feel just right!

Whimsical Wandering

With a skip, I roam through streets of whim,
Chasing shadows on a playful whim.
Umbrellas dance, flapping in the breeze,
As I twirl round corners, giggling with ease.

Puddles sparkle, inviting a leap,
Each splash a secret, the world so deep.
A squirrel in a bowtie nods with flair,
Says, 'Jump right in, it's beyond compare!'

Through gardens of laughter, down lanes of cheer,
I find every corner, magic is near.
With whimsical signs that giggle and tease,
I wander freely, tickled by the breeze.

So come along, let's dance and parade,
In a world where the silly won't ever fade.
With every step, let's turn up the fun,
In this joyful journey, for everyone!

The Secrets of the Verdant Realm

In the garden where giggles grow,
Flowers whisper secrets, don't you know?
Worms wear spectacles, clever and wise,
While ants parade under butterfly skies.

Chirping crickets play jazz on a leaf,
The beetles dance, oh what a belief!
Grasshoppers hopping to a silly tune,
As sunbeams laugh at the antics of noon.

Threads of Nature's Mystique

Snails in tuxedos slide with great flair,
While ladybugs giggle without a care.
The vines gossip with a tickling breeze,
Painting the air with their silly tease.

Mushrooms wearing hats, a quirky sight,
They throw a party every starry night.
Caterpillars curl, then dance with glee,
In the patchwork of whimsy, oh, how free!

Serenade of the Vibrant Green

Dandelions puff like marshmallows bright,
While squirrels compose a symphony at night.
Toads croon ballads, their voices so grand,
As the moon winks down on the merry band.

Twirling petals pirouette in the sun,
Chasing each other, oh what funny fun!
Nature's laughter echoes with delight,
In the symphony of the starry night.

Under the Umbrella of Nature's Palette

The trees wear colors, a splendid array,
As squirrels plot mischief and playful fray.
Breezes brush cheeks like a tickling friend,
While flowers declare, "Come and play till the end!"

In the shade of laughter, shadows dance free,
Grass blades gossip like best friends at tea.
Each leaf in chorus sings joyful and bright,
Nature's own party, what a wonderful sight!

www.ingramcontent.com/pod-product-compliance
Lightning Source LLC
Chambersburg PA
CBHW072148200426
43209CB00051B/839